D1406251

DESIGN CHALLENGE:
Half Log Cabin Plus!

BY SHARYN CRAIG

CHITRA PUBLICATIONS
Your Best Value in Quilting

746.46
CRA

Copyright ©1998 by Sharyn Craig
All Rights Reserved. Published in the United States of America.
Printed in Hong Kong.

Chitra Publications
2 Public Avenue
Montrose, Pennsylvania, 18801

No part of this publication may be reproduced or transmitted in any form or by any means, electronic or mechanical, including photocopy, recording, or any information storage and retrieval system now known or to be invented, without permission in writing from the publisher, except by a reviewer who wishes to quote brief passages in connection with a review written for inclusion in a magazine, newspaper, or broadcast.

First Printing: 1998

Library of Congress Cataloging-in-Publication Data

Craig, Sharyn, 1947-
    Design challenge : half log cabin plus! / by Sharyn Craig.
        p. cm.
    ISBN 1-885588-20-8
      1. Patchwork.   2. Patchwork--Patterns.   3. Quilting.   4. Quilting--Patterns.
5. Log cabin quilts.   I. Title.   II. Title: Half log cabin plus!
    TT835.C718 1998
    746.46'041--DC21   98-21878
                         CIP

Editor: Nancy Roberts
Design and Illustrations: Susan Barefoot
Cover Photography: Guy Cali Associates, Inc., Clarks Summit, PA
Inside Photography: Ken Jacques Photography, San Diego, CA; Craige's Photography, Montrose, PA; and Van Zandbergen Photography, Brackney, PA.

Quilts on the front cover were made by Carolyn Smith (Top Left),
Katie Hargrave (Top Center), Sally Graessel (Top Right), and Sharyn Craig (Bottom).

Quilts on the back cover were made by Carol Rhodes (Top),
Mike Tagg (Center) and Sharyn Craig (Bottom).

Our Mission Statement:
We publish quality quilting magazines and books that recognize, promote and inspire self-expression. We are dedicated to serving our customers with respect, kindness and efficiency.

I'm thrilled that you're going to try this fun and easy way to liven up your quilts with Half Log Cabin Plus. This block is a spin-off design from the block used to make the scrappy Half Log Cabin quilts featured in my book *Design Challenge: Half Log Cabin Quilts* (Chitra Publications, 1996). Half Log Cabin Plus blocks have small triangles running diagonally through their centers. These triangles add extra zip to the blocks and give you a chance to introduce a color accent to them. I think of Half Log Cabin Plus as more than plain old logs.

The design came about when my friend and former student Carolyn Smith asked if adding a diagonal row of triangles through the center of the Half Log Cabin block was possible. She liked the effect when she saw it done using traditional Log Cabin blocks and wanted to achieve it with the Half Log Cabin ones as well. Carolyn's question piqued my interest. I was sure the triangles could be added to the pattern, but how could it be done using an easy and organized sewing system?

It took making many quilts and teaching dozens of workshops to refine the sewing system so that you'll be able to stitch Half Log Cabin Plus blocks quickly and efficiently. I share that system in the following pages with step-by-step photos and diagrams. The quilts are wonderfully fun and so easy to make.

The photos are intended to inspire you with visual stimulation. They are not "written-in-stone-recipes." I suggest that you look at the block layouts in the quilts to discover the ones you find most pleasing. Notice the colors used for the triangles that run through the blocks, too. I refer to the fabric used for them as control fabric. Some quilts have strong, brightly colored triangles, while others have subdued colors for a more subtle effect. Which look appeals to you more? Ask yourself questions like this as you review the quilts. Your answers will guide you toward developing your own design.

You can make your quilt in a random, scrappy style or use a controlled color scheme. I recommend working in the scrap format when you begin, though. This way you won't run out of fabric no matter how big you make your quilt because the logs don't have to match. You simply cut more strips and keep on piecing! The instructions in this book are for using 2"-wide strips, but you can work with any width strips you wish. Quiltmaker Ruth Gordy likes making Half Log Cabin Plus in miniature, so there are even bonus patterns for 2" and 3" foundation-pieced blocks.

Depending on how much time you have, you can even work on the blocks a few at a time. The directions are for 24 blocks, but you'll see how easy it is to make any number you wish.

Let's get started. Gather your fabrics, cutter and mat and prepare for some sewing fun as you make blocks, blocks and more blocks! Be warned that sewing these blocks is every bit as addictive as sewing those for Half Log Cabin quilts. Once you get started, you won't want to stop!

Sharyn

CONTENTS

CHAPTER 1

CHOOSING FABRICS

The instructions provided are for 6" finished blocks. Contrast between the two halves of the block is important, so use a variety of dark and light print fabrics. When you study the Half Log Cabin Plus block, you'll notice that it is made from three light pieces, four dark pieces and four triangles made from a control fabric.

I recommend making Half Log Cabin Plus blocks using 2"-wide strips when you begin. If you work in a scrappy format and use a variety of fabrics for the logs, you won't even need to know in advance how big your quilt will be. The beauty of scrappy Half Log Cabin Plus quilts is that you can never run out of a fabric you need for the logs because they don't need to match. If you begin to make a 24-block baby quilt but like the blocks so much that you decide to make a king-size quilt instead, just cut more 2"-wide strips and keep sewing!

Each selvage-to-selvage dark strip will yield enough pieces for two blocks while each light strip will yield enough for up to four blocks. For more variety (fewer repeats), work with shorter strips of fabric, cutting only enough for one block from any one fabric. As a guideline, 2" x 18" strips are a generous but not wasteful size with which to work for dark logs. Similarly, 2" x 12" strips work for light ones.

OPTIONS FOR LIGHT STRIPS

When you study your fabric stash, are you concerned about having enough variety in light prints to make these blocks? Often quilters have many dark prints but fewer light ones. If so, you may wish to use just one light print in all of the blocks. Or use three different light prints, keeping the position of each one the same in every block. Some examples can be found on page 12 and the front cover.

If you choose either of these options though, be sure that you have enough of the single print or the three prints to avoid running out of fabric if you decide to make a bigger quilt. Use the Yardage Guideline Chart to determine how much fabric you need for each of these options.

A third option is to look at the wrong sides of your fabrics. Many that are not light enough when you look at the right side make wonderful light prints when using the wrong side. If it bothers you to use the wrong side of a fabric, remember that you paid just as much for it as you did the right side!

OPTIONS FOR THE CONTROL FABRIC

This fabric will be used for the small triangles that run through the block diagonally. The brighter and more intense the control fabric, the more visible it will be in the finished blocks. Visualize an antique Log Cabin quilt. Do you picture the blocks with red or yellow center squares that were frequently used? We think of red and yellow as bright accent colors. When making Half Log Cabin Plus blocks, you may want the triangles to be accents that sparkle in the design. If so, select a bright control fabric.

Depending on the effect you are trying to create, you might not want the triangles to be "strong" or "bright." You can get an interesting effect by choosing a light control fabric. It can cause the triangles to seem

---

YARDAGE GUIDELINE CHART

When using one light fabric for all of the blocks:
- One 2"-wide strip cut from selvage to selvage yields enough pieces for four blocks.

When using three light fabrics and keeping the position of each one the same in all of the blocks:
- One 2"-wide strip cut selvage to selvage and then cut into 2" squares yields enough pieces for 16 blocks. These are used in

Position #1.
- One 2"-wide strip cut selvage to selvage and then cut into 2" x 3 1/2" rectangles yields enough pieces for 12 blocks. These are used in Position #2.
- One 2"-wide strip cut selvage to selvage and then cut into 2" x 5" rectangles yields enough pieces for 8 blocks. These are used in Position #3.

to disappear, yet it still creates a bold graphic quality in the blocks. Katie Hargrave's "Patriot Games" on page 13 illustrates this concept.

If you opt for purple, blue, green or another dark color for the control fabric, then maintain contrast by eliminating strips of that color for the logs. The goal is to make blocks that look divided diagonally into light and dark halves with a little extra visual "flavor" supplied by the control fabric triangles.

Whatever control fabric you chose, each 2"-wide strip cut selvage to selvage yields enough pieces for about four blocks. Knowing this will help you determine how much control fabric you need. About 3/8 yard of fabric will be enough for 24 blocks.

CHAPTER 2

CUTTING AND SEWING BLOCK PARTS

To learn the sewing system, begin by making 24 Half Log Cabin Plus blocks. Set them in six rows of four blocks each to make a crib-size quilt that measures 24" x 36" without borders. You can add to this number of blocks later if you decide to make a larger quilt. The cutting directions are for this number of blocks but you can make fewer blocks at one time if you prefer. I often like to make sets of eight, but any multiple of four will work. Here's what you'll need to get started.

MATERIALS
• Fabrics (control fabric, assorted dark prints and one or more light prints as described in Chapter 1)
• Rotary cutter and mat
• Strip-cutting ruler (NOTE: *I recommend a 6" x 12" ruler.*)
• 1/4"-wide masking tape
• Sewing machine

PREPARATION
• Cut 6: 2" x 44" strips, control

fabric
• Cut 24: 2" x 18" strips, different dark prints
• Cut 24: 2" x 12" strips, different light prints*
• To simplify cutting these strips into pieces for the blocks, adhere a length of 1/4"-wide masking tape along the length of the strip cutting ruler. Then mark the tape at these increments: 2", 3 1/2", 5" and 6 1/2". I suggest using a permanent-ink pen. Because the logs are cut in various lengths, I find I'm less likely to

make a mistake when I use these marks as a guide.

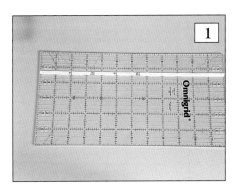

*ALTERNATE PREPARATION FOR LIGHT PRINTS

If you are using a single light print or three light prints, both options described in Chapter 1, use these instructions for 24 blocks:

For one light print:
Cut 6: 2" x 44" strips, light print

For three light prints:
Cut 2: 2" x 44" strips, first light print for position #1
Cut 3: 2" x 44" strips, second light print for position #2
Cut 3: 2" x 44" strips, third light print for position #3

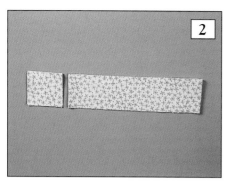

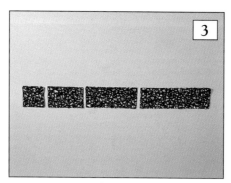

CUTTING

All dimensions include a 1/4" seam allowance.

For the control fabric:

• Fold a 2" x 44" control fabric in quarters and trim one end to even it, removing the selvages and the fold. Cut it into 2" squares. Because the fabric is folded this way, each cut will make enough squares (4) for one block. Depending on the usable width of your fabric, you may get four or five cuts from a strip. Repeat with the remaining strips, cutting enough 2" squares (96) for 24 blocks.

For the dark print strips:

• Stack 8 different 2" x 18" dark print strips, right side up. Even the ends.

• Cutting through all eight layers and using the 2" mark on the tape as a guide, cut 2" squares from the stack. Set these 8 squares aside.

• Move the ruler and cut 2" x 3 1/2" rectangles from the stack, using the 3 1/2" guideline on the tape. Set these 8 rectangles aside.

• Repeat, cutting 2" x 5" and 2" x 6 1/2" rectangles from the stack. You will have 8 of each size.

• In the same manner, cut squares and rectangles from the remaining dark print strips, stacking same-size pieces on top of those previously cut and setting them aside.

• Work with one stack of shapes at a time and follow these instructions to scramble the dark print rectangles for random placement of fabrics in the blocks. Remove one 2" x 3 1/2" rectangle from the top of the stack and place it on the bottom. Remove the top two 2" x 5" rectangles from the stack and place them on the bottom. Remove the top three 2" x 6 1/2" rectangles from the stack and place them on the bottom. Each stack contains 24 rectangles, but now they are in a different order.

2" x 2"	Do not scramble
2" x 3 1/2"	Move 1 from top to bottom
2" x 5"	Move 2 from top to bottom
2" x 6 1/2"	Move 3 from top to bottom

For the light print strips:

Instructions are for using a variety of light prints which need to be scrambled as you did the dark ones. If you are using a single light print or three light prints for your blocks, follow the instructions in the box.

• Stack 8 different 2" x 12" light print strips, right side up. Even the ends.

• Cutting through all eight layers and using the 2" mark on the tape as a guide, cut 2" squares from the stack. Set these 8 squares aside.

• Move the ruler and cut 2" x 3 1/2" and then 2" x 5" rectangles from the stack, using the guidelines on the tape. You will have 8 of each size.

• In the same manner, cut squares and rectangles from the remaining light print strips, stacking same-size pieces on top of those previously cut.

• Scramble the light print rectangles as you did the dark ones.

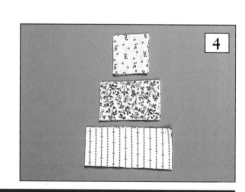

ALTERNATE CUTTING FOR LIGHT PRINTS

For one light print:

• Place four strips folded in half on top of each other with folds at one end and selvages at the other. Even the selvage ends, trimming off the selvages. Measure and cut 2" squares, 2" x 3 1/2" rectangles and 2" x 5" rectangles. Repeat to cut these three shapes from the strips again.

2"	3 1/2"	5"	2"	3 1/2"	5"	◄ Fold

For three light prints:

• Leave strips folded in fourths. Cut 2" squares from the first light print strip. Cut 2" x 3 1/2" rectangles from the second light print strip. Cut 2" x 5" rectangles from the third light print strip. You need 24 of each shape.

2"	2"	2"	2"	2"

3 1/2"	3 1/2"	◄ Folds

5"	5"

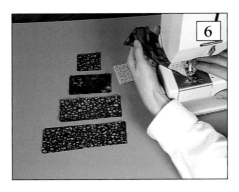

SEWING THE CONTROL FABRIC TRIANGLES ON DARK LOGS:

• Place the stacks of dark squares and rectangles near your sewing machine from smallest to largest, with the largest stack closest to you.

• Place a stack of 2" control fabric squares near your sewing machine where they will be easily accessible.

• Beginning with the stack of largest rectangles, pick up one rectangle and place a 2" control fabric square on the end closest to you, right sides together and edges aligned. Noting the direction of the seamline, stitch the square to the rectangle by sewing diagonally from corner to corner. You can eyeball this seamline or see TIPS on page 8 for techniques to ensure accuracy. Leave the presser foot down and the stitched unit in the machine. Do not clip threads.

• Pick up the next rectangle from the same stack and place a 2" control fabric square on it. Chain sew by feeding it into the machine right after the first one. Continue chain sewing control fabric squares to the remaining rectangles in this stack.

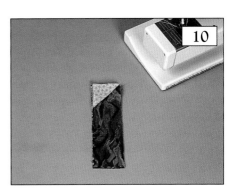

• Remove the units from the machine, clipping threads close to the last unit sewn. Place them on the work surface so that the first unit sewn is at the left and the last is at the right.

• Beginning at the left, clip the units apart and stack them so that the first unit sewn is at the bottom of the stack.

• Pick up the top unit and finger press the control fabric square toward the corner, forming three layers in one corner. Set it aside on the work surface. Continue finger pressing one unit at a time, stacking them so that now the last unit sewn is on the bottom and the first one sewn in on the top again.

• Repeat, sewing control fabric squares to all of the remaining dark print rectangles and squares and maintaining the order of the stacks. Now you have all the pieces you need to assemble the blocks.

To reduce bulk for quilting:
• You may wish to trim away one or both layers of fabric beneath each control fabric.

To avoid waste and make small pieced squares for another project:
• You may wish to stitch each square again before cutting the units apart. To do this, sew 1/2" away from the first seamline and toward the corner of each unit. Then trim between the two seamlines, 1/4" away from each. Set the small pieced squares aside for another project. Clip the other units apart. Open, press and stack as described.

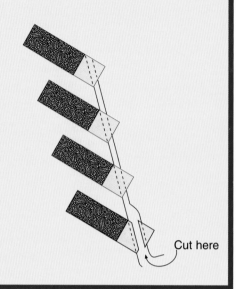

Cut here

TIPS

TRY THESE METHODS FOR GREATER ACCURACY. THE THIRD ONE IS MY FAVORITE

Crease a sewing line:
• Fold control fabric squares corner to corner and make a diagonal crease. Use the crease as the sewing line.

Mark a sewing line:
• Lightly draw a sewing line from corner to corner on the wrong side of each control square.

Make a guideline:
• Use a guideline made from 1/4"-wide masking tape adhered to the throat plate of your machine and aligned with the needle. To do this, lower the needle, leaving the presser foot up. Position a strip-cutting ruler against the needle from the left side. Lower the presser foot to secure the ruler.
• Place a strip of 1/4"-wide masking tape

on the throat plate of the machine ahead of the needle, snugly against the right edge of the ruler.

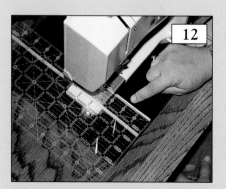

• Lift the needle and the presser foot. Then remove the ruler.
• When sewing, line up two opposite corners of each control square with the left edge of

the tape. Keep your eye on the corner of the control square you are feeding into the machine rather than on the needle. You'll get perfect corner to corner sewing every time!

8

CHAPTER 3

SEWING THE BLOCKS

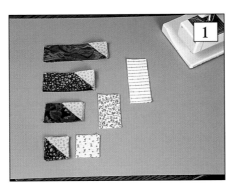

Lay out the stacks so they are arranged to look like a block. Position each stack of logs so that the control triangles "march" from lower left to upper right. Look through the units in each stack to be sure all of the control triangles are sewn in the correct direction. Because this is a directional block, you'll spot any incorrectly sewn ones easily. If so, correct them now. If, while you sew, you find a repeat fabric in a block despite scrambling the logs, simply exchange the piece with another in the stack.

Once you have determined that all of the pieces are the ones you want to use, you're ready to sew blocks. Study the numbered diagram for sewing order. Notice that for seam #1, the dark print pieced square is on the left while the light square is on the right. In all of the sewing, pieces on the right will be placed on top of pieces on the left.

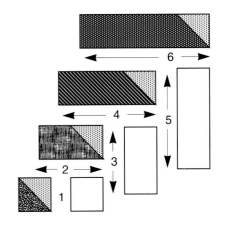

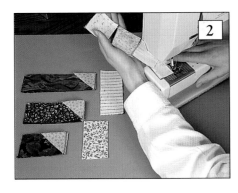

- Place the light square (right) on the dark pieced square (left), right sides together and edges aligned. Sew them and leave them in the machine with the presser foot down while you prepare the next pair for chain sewing.
- Chain sew the remaining units in the stack.

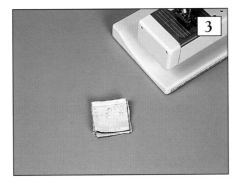

- Using the same method you used when stitching the control triangles, remove the units from the machine and place them on the work surface so that the first unit sewn is at the left. Keep the "newest" fabric (the piece added last) on the top—in this case the light square. Beginning at the left, clip the units apart and stack them so that the first unit sewn is at the bottom of the stack.

- Pick up the top unit and finger press the seam allowance toward the light square. NOTE: *In each step, press seam allowances away from the center pieced square.* Place it on the work surface, right side up. Continue finger pressing one unit at a time, stacking them so that now the last unit sewn is on the bottom and the first sewn is on the top again.

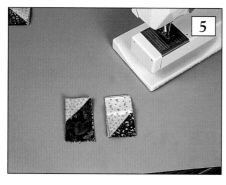

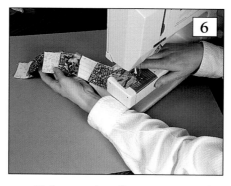

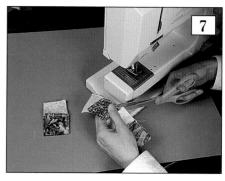

• Position the stack of these pieced units with the fabric added last (the light square) at the top. Place the stack of second dark logs to the left.

• Pick up the first unit in the stack at the right, place it on the first unit in the stack at the left and sew them together. Leaving these units in the machine, chain sew the remaining units in these stacks.

• Remove them from the machine and place them on the work surface. Clip and stack the units as before.

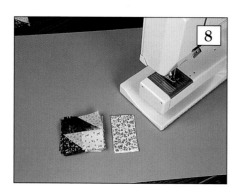

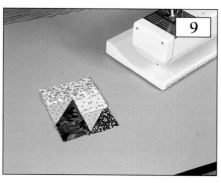

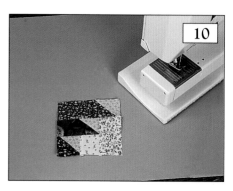

• Finger press each unit, remembering to press seam allowances away from the center square, and stack them as before. Keep the fabric added last (in this case the dark log) at the top.

• Place this stack of units on the left. Place the stack of 2" x 3 1/2" light print rectangles at the right. (HINT: Light is always on the right when the new fabric to be added is light!)

• Chain sew these units and rectangles as before, remembering to place the one at the right on top of the one at the left.

• Clip, stack, finger press and stack again, keeping the fabric added last (in this case, the light rectangle) at the top.

• Continue sewing all of the logs in the stacks, following the numbered seam sequence, until the blocks are completed.

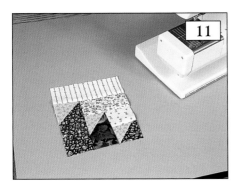

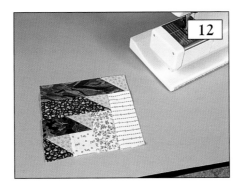

- Press the blocks and get ready for some design fun.

TIPS

HELPFUL HINTS TO REMEMBER

- Always position units with the newest fabric (last piece added) at the top.
- When adding a light log, always place it on the right. Right = light. (Light/Right rhymes. The rhyme will help you remember.)
- When adding a dark log, always place it on the left. Left = dark. (This saying will help you remember: "Don't be left in the dark.")
- Keep the log on the right on top while sewing.
- Keep proper fabric order by always placing chained units on the work surface with the first sewn unit at the left. Begin clipping and stacking from the left (first sewn is on the bottom of the stack). Reverse the order by finger pressing and restacking each unit, beginning at the top of the stack (last sewn) and ending with the bottom of the stack (first sewn).

Bonus:
Full-Size Foundation Patterns for Miniature Half Log Cabin Plus Blocks

3" BLOCK

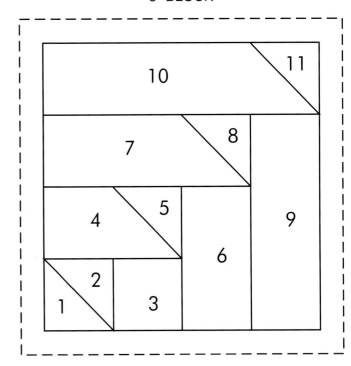

2" BLOCK

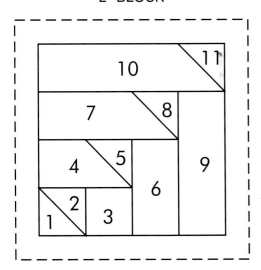

CHAPTER 4

LOGS PLUS GALLERY

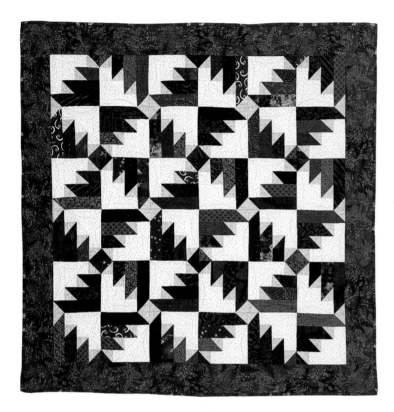

◄

*I chose a single light print, assorted blue prints and soft yellow control fabric for **"Pinwheel Logs"** (42" square). Half Log Cabin Plus blocks are so versatile!*

►

*What if you used only one light print in the blocks and set the blocks on point? That's what I did in **"Point of Order"** (58" square).*

◄ A lone pine stands in the center of Terry Shepard's **"With a Little Help from My Friends"** *(44" square). The turquoise control fabric triangles accent the blocks in a subtle way.*

► Helen Jacobsen achieved a diamond look in the regular rows of **"On the March"** *(72" x 84"). The innovative pieced outer border echoes the colors and fabrics used in the quilt center. I think the quilt has a strong, masculine feel.*

◄ *Interesting angles appear in a Half Log Cabin Plus design when the control fabric triangles are cut from a light print. Katie Hargrave explored this idea in her delightful **"Patriot Games"** (42" square).*

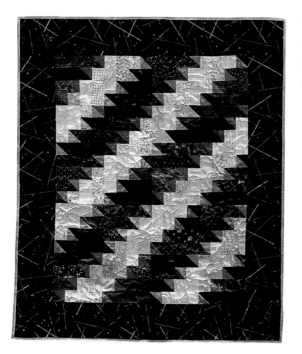

▲

*Look what happens when you use several different control fabrics! My Half Log Cabin Plus blocks are set in a simple Field and Furrows setting in "**At Play in the Fields**" (34" x 40"), but the quilt has a vibrant look thanks to the spark added by assorted bright triangles.*

▲

*Carolyn Smith, whose construction question prompted the Half Log Cabin Plus Design Challenge, made "**Plaid Persuasion**" (38" square). Carolyn made the blocks larger (7 1/2") by stitching four light and five dark logs in each one.*

◄

*Elaine Berg added more positions to her Half Log Cabin Plus blocks in order to make "**Barn Raising with a Twist**" (60" square) without making a lot more blocks.*

▶ Any 6" block can be used with the Half Log Cabin Plus blocks to create a lively design like **"Star Bright"** (66" square) stitched by Jill Schneider. Jill appliquéd stars on Snowball blocks and combined them with Half Log Cabin Plus blocks in a Fields and Furrows set. Notice that she used two different control fabrics for the triangles.

◀ Joan Hodgebloom created this asymmetrical look by joining blocks in a spiraling Barn Raising set. Study the dark prints Joan used in **"Creative Spiral"** (52" x 40"), choose one and find it wherever it appears in the quilt. It's easy to see that while fabrics may be repeated in the blocks, they always occupy different positions. The scrambling step ensures that this works.

▶

Cher Chu played "what if… ?" with her Half Log Cabin Plus blocks and came up with this awesome answer. Rather than splitting the blocks into half-dark/half-light, Cher repeated fabrics on both sides. She created a gradated chevron look which undulates across **"Amber Waves"** *(58" square). Notice that Cher also added a fifth position in every block.*

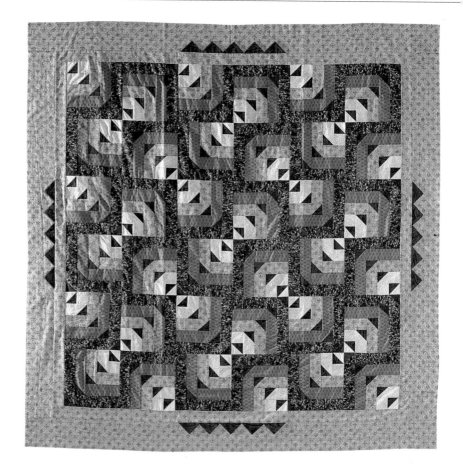

▲

Ruth Gordy loves miniatures. She made **"Little Logs Plus"** *(17" square), a tiny version of Half Log Cabin Plus using the foundation-piecing method. You'll find foundation patterns for 2" and 3" blocks on page 11 so you can try your hand at making little quilts like Ruth's.*

▶

Kathy Amparan played with Half Log Cabin Plus blocks and came up with this innovative setting for **"Logs Surround"** *(46" x 58"). She carefully cut fabric strips from a border print to capture the motif for the narrow inner border and repeated the control fabric color in the wide outer border.*